TEN LAWS
for
SUCCESS

PAT
ROBERTSON

Most Charisma House Book Group products are available at special quantity discounts for bulk purchase for sales promotions, premiums, fund-raising, and educational needs. For details, call us at (407) 333-0600 or visit our website at www.charismahouse.com.

TEN LAWS FOR SUCCESS by Pat Robertson
Published by Charisma House
Charisma Media/Charisma House Book Group
600 Rinehart Road, Lake Mary, Florida 32746

Visit the author's website at PatRobertson.com.

Library of Congress Cataloging-in-Publication Data:
An application to register this book for cataloging has been
submitted to the Library of Congress.
International Standard Book Number: 978-1-62999-870-1
E-book ISBN: 978-1-62999-871-8

Portions of this book were previously published by Pat Robertson
as *The Secret Kingdom (revised edition)*, ISBN 978-0-99861-571-4,
copyright © 2017. (Original edition published by W Pub Group,
ISBN 978-0-84991-004-3, copyright © 1992.)

20 21 22 23 24 — 9 8 7 6 5 4 3 2 1
Printed in the United States of America

CONTENTS

PREFACE

So I turned my mind to understand, to investigate
and to search out wisdom and the scheme of things.

—ECCLESIASTES 7:25, NIV

AFTER THE DARK days of the Nixon administration, the scandal of Watergate, and the resignation of a president, the American people were looking for a fresh start. They found it in the person of a former governor of Georgia who proclaimed that he was a born-again Christian. Jimmy Carter was a Sunday school teacher, a longtime member of a small Baptist church, and a person who said that he wanted to be as decent as the American people.

In 1976 I traveled to Jimmy Carter's home in Plains, Georgia, and sat with him on his outside terrace for an interview for my television program, *The 700 Club*. We talked about domestic issues, the situation of the farmers, the concept of détente with the Russians, and a wide range of social and political issues. In closing, I asked then Governor Carter if he intended to have born-again Christians in his administration. Up to this point his answers had been quite forthright. The answer to the last question was somewhat vague.

Lou Sheldon, one of our faculty members, was quite close to Jimmy Carter. I asked Lou to ask then President-Elect Carter if he would welcome some suggestions for his official governing team. He replied in the affirmative, so Lou and

I went to work compiling a list of faithful Democrats who were distinguished in business or philanthropy and who would make strong candidates for government positions. We put together a list of ten or fifteen such individuals and then had them thoroughly vetted by a friend of mine who held a high position in the Civil Service Commission.

It was a beautiful presentation, carefully annotated, offering candidates that any president would be pleased to have in his administration. Lou flew down to Georgia and drove from the airport to Carter's home in Plains. He found the future president barefoot and in blue jeans with none of the aura of prestige and power.

Carter took the list that had been prepared, read it carefully, and then began to cry. When Lou told me about it, he remarked, "Jimmy was so touched by the work that we had done in preparing this list, he began to cry."

I knew otherwise. I said, "Lou, he didn't cry because we worked so hard. He cried because he's already given his administration over to David Rockefeller and the Trilateral Commission." Regrettably I was right. The big-money people had backed Carter, and they had engineered the success of his campaign. He was indebted to them. When he announced his cabinet, it was loaded with members of the Council of Foreign Relations, the Trilateral Commission, and other Rockefeller entities.

Since I had invested so much effort to gain success for a born-again Christian, I then took a keen interest in how government works. I also was able to see firsthand a series of policy blunders that had devastating consequences for the United States and the world.

Just to name a few, consider this: In the late '70s, President Carter considered the shah of Iran to be our strong friend and ally. Regrettably, he had oppressed his people with the secret police known as the SAVAK. When the people began to riot, the shah called the president of the United States and asked for help. President Carter initially offered asylum to the shah, but after realizing how intensely the Iranian people wanted to overthrow him, Carter withdrew. Shortly thereafter, a revolution did take place, and the Ayatollah Ruhollah Khomeini flew in from Europe to the cheers of millions and proceeded to establish a Muslim theocracy in Iran that referred to the United States as the "Great Satan."

In Africa, the people of Zimbabwe held a free election and chose a Methodist bishop, Abel Muzorewa, as their president. The Carter administration refused to acknowledge the free election of a Christian man and instead insisted on supporting a warlord named Robert Mugabe as president of that nation.[1] Mugabe recently died after a brutal tenure of office that decimated his country.

In Angola, leftist forces were supported by ten thousand Cuban troops, and Carter's administration declared the presence of ten thousand Communist troops in that country as a "stabilizing force."[2]

Perhaps the greatest humiliation of President Carter's administration came when a gang of ruffians overran our embassy in Tehran, and President Carter retreated to the Rose Garden in an attempt to show solidarity with the suffering of our captive workers in that Muslim country.[3] It was no surprise, therefore, in light of a period that had been called a malaise by the president,[4] that the cowboy from California won an overwhelming victory in the general election and retired Jimmy Carter to his peanut farm and to his work building houses with Habitat for Humanity.

I watched all of these events unfold with an eager cry to the Lord, "God, please show me how the world works and how it is supposed to work." As I prayed this prayer, the strong revelation came to me. Jesus Christ is God, and whatever He says carries the authority of the Creator of the universe. I began to understand that when Jesus spoke without regard to the composition of the audience or the time or the place, His words on general subjects had the same authority as the physical laws, such as the law of gravity. There exists what I call a secret kingdom. It is unknown—but known. It is not obvious on the surface of things but is underlying everything. So my quest was to find out the laws of the secret kingdom that Jesus Christ had enunciated and to see how they pertained to human growth and development, to social organization, to politics, and to the affairs of nations. Out of these revelations I was able to glean a list of ten overriding principles that I believe govern the success or failure of each human and every human organization. I call them the Ten Laws of Success.

CHAPTER 1

THE LAW OF USE

S O, LET'S BEGIN with the most important law that governs individual growth and development. I call it the Law of Use. My understanding springs from a parable that Jesus gave known as the parable of the talents.[1]

In this parable Jesus recounts the story of a nobleman who was going away to a far country to receive a kingdom. Before he left, he wanted his officials to be occupied in his affairs, and so he gave to each of the three a sum of money with the instructions, "Occupy till I come."[2]

To one of his officials he gave five talents. This official took what had been given to him and began to use it wisely. He bought goods and then took them up to Syria, where he sold them at a profit. He then took that profit and bought goods in Syria, which he took back home and once again sold at a profit. As he continued to use the talents that had been given to him, the funds under his care doubled in value.

The same scenario unfolded for the man who had been given two talents. He bought, he sold, and he traded. He made small and large profits, and at the end of his term he had doubled his master's money.

The third servant was more cautious. He hated risks, and he was afraid of taking losses. He said to himself, "My master is a hard man. He gathers where he has not sown, and he reaps where he has not scattered seed. I will not lose any of his money. Instead, I will wrap it tightly in a bag and then bury the bag in the ground. When my master returns, I can show him that I have lost absolutely not one penny of his money."[3]

At the appointed time the nobleman, now crowned king, called his servants to him to determine how they had fared with his money. The one who had received the five talents came happily before the king and spread out ten talents. "I have taken your money, my lord, and have doubled it during your absence." To this the lord replied, "Well done, good and faithful servant; you were faithful over a few things, I will make you ruler over many things. Enter into the joy of your lord."[4]

The second servant came before him and proudly announced that the two talents had been doubled. To this the king replied, "Well done, good and faithful servant; you have been faithful over a few things, I will make you ruler over many things. Enter into the joy of your lord."[5]

The third servant appeared before the king and said, "I knew that you were a hard man... that you reaped where you did not sow and gathered where you did not scatter. I was afraid. Therefore, I took your money, buried it in the ground, and have dug it up. Here is your money. I have not lost a single cent."[6] At this, the king was irate. "You wicked and slothful servant," he said. "You at least should have given my money to the exchangers so that when I returned, I would have received my own plus interest." And to the amazement of the audience, he said,

"Take the talent from this servant and give it to the one who has ten talents."[7]

This statement flew in the face of what the audience thought was fair, but this is how the kingdom of God works according to the word of the Son of God. "To him who has, more will be given. And he that has not, even what he thinks he has will be taken away from him."[8] Fair or not, this is the way God set up His plan for human growth and development.

However, just ponder this statement. Jesus called the servant who did not use what had been given to him "wicked and slothful."[9] The overly cautious person who does not use fully what has been given him considers himself prudent. Jesus calls him wicked and slothful.

Think how this plays out in our modern world. Millions of people are gripped by fear, and they put their savings into bank accounts that generally yield 0.09 percent, according to FDIC data.[10] These returns, laughably enough, are actually subject to taxation. Yet hundreds of millions of American people think they are being prudent when they sink their money into this losing proposition—so they can proudly tell their friends that they keep their reserves in a "safe bank account."

They might as well have dug a hole in the ground and put their dollars in the ground. They are not good stewards. They are wicked and slothful at a time when any number of AAA-rated stocks and bonds are yielding anywhere from 4 to 9 percent.

Think of the crushing burdens that come in life from

those who refuse to take chances and to exercise what has been given to them. Young men and women with great talent are afraid to move on into college or a profession because they want to play it safe. Think of the young woman with a sparkling personality and a potentially glorious future who marries some dull soul because he has money and the marriage would be safe. Think of the brilliant inventor who doesn't bring forth concepts that God gives him because he is afraid to take a risk. Think of the employee who turns down a job opportunity because he is afraid to leave familiar surroundings and would rather play it safe.

For that matter, think what would have happened to America if pioneering families had been afraid to push from the Mississippi to take advantage of the opportunities opened up for them by the vast expanse of the West. In fact, where would America be if brave sailors had not left the security of their homeland to sail across unchartered waters in search of new opportunities? Those who refused to take any risks did not see the blessing of the Law of Use, and Jesus called them "wicked and slothful."[11] An early divine said that people will be judged on the basis not of what they did but on what they could have done if they had availed themselves of the spiritual anointing and opportunity that God gave them.

Marian Anderson, the famous Metropolitan Opera soloist, was approached by a young woman who said, "I'd give my right arm if I could sing like you." To that, Marian replied, "Would you give eight hours practice a day?"[12]

The great pianist Ignacy Jan Paderewski said, "If I miss one day of practice, I notice it. If I miss two days, the critics notice it. If I miss three days, the audience notices it."[13]

CONSIDER THE PHYSICAL REALM

If an athlete exercises his or her muscles day after day, he or she will grow much stronger muscles. If, on the other hand, he or she would bind an arm to the side for a period of six or eight months, that arm would be so weak that it would be impossible for the person to lift even a coffee cup.

In terms of knowledge, a student who practices arithmetic can move into geometry. And if he or she practices geometry faithfully, he or she can move into calculus. And if he or she practices calculus faithfully, then it would be possible to move into higher mathematics.

The human heart is essentially a pump that sends oxygenated blood and nutrients throughout the human body. One part of the heart is known as the ventricles; the other is known as the atria. Doctors who specialize in the care of the heart are called cardiologists. However, later advances in the science of the heart have revealed electrical pulses that control certain aspects of the heart's functioning. This specialty is referred to as electrophysiology. As blood flows into the heart, the atria push it to the ventricles, which in turn circulate oxygenated blood to the lungs and throughout the body.

As people grow older, the upper parts of the heart begin to malfunction. The term used to describe this condition is *atrial fibrillation* or *atrial flutter*. It's hard to describe the fatigue that comes over an individual who suffers from this condition. Yet millions of people have it—and I was one of those people.

My local cardiologist recommended a series of standard medications, which had the effect of slowing my heart down and leaving me in a dopey condition. I went to the Cleveland Clinic, noted for its heart health program, to see if they could relieve my condition. Their solution was to insert a type of electrode through one of the arteries in my groin up into my heart. And then, using very complex machinery, they pinpointed portions of my heart that were sending out errant electrical impulses. In order to kill or ablate these impulses, I endured two of these painful ablation sessions over a period of months, but both were unsuccessful.

Finally, at my area hospital I was able to contact technicians who could perform what is known as a cardioversion. The principle of this technique is to shock the heart to make it begin to function in what is called "sinus rhythm." I was required to fast from water and food for at least six hours, then had an IV inserted into one of my veins, into which was then inserted Propofol, what is laughingly called the "milk of amnesia."

Two electric plates were placed on the front and back of my chest, and after I was unconscious, 600 joules of electricity were applied to the electrodes, which in turn shocked my heart back into normal rhythm. I was blissfully free from the atrial fibrillation that had zapped so much of my strength.

I was able to live like a normal human being for about half a year; then the atrial fibrillation came back again with the same incredible fatigue, so I was back in the hospital for another cardioversion under what we began to call the "Pat Zapper." Unfortunately the atrial fibrillation came back more and more frequently until the attending electrophysiologist said to me, "This is a chronic disease, and it will continue to return. I recommend a pacemaker." The problem with getting a pacemaker, at least in the old days, was that it was very serious; the AV node in the heart is cut, and the heart then relies on a battery pack inserted into the chest. If there is a short in the battery pack, there's no backup, and the patient dies.

To allay my fears, my doctor explained that the electrical system in the current pacemakers carries a level of redundancy, and I need not worry about an electrical short. He told me that a flap of skin over my chest muscle would be lifted, and a small battery pack would be sewn in place with leads attached directly into my heart muscle.

I asked him who in our area was able to perform such an operation. He replied, "I can do it," to which I asked, "How many of these have you done?" His reply: "I have successfully done 2,300." If he had said, "This is the first one," I would have thanked him for his kindness and asked for a second opinion. However, because of his experience, I trusted him with the surgery. I had the pacemaker installed in my chest. And now, several years after the

surgery, my heart is pumping like brand-new, and I've had
no discomfort whatsoever.

Some years ago I took flying lessons and received a private pilot's license. After several flights, I read that the vast
majority of airplane accidents with private planes involve
pilots that were flying less than ten hours a year.

As a fledgling pilot, I was given a checklist before
I started the engines and began to take off. In the old
piston planes, I had to check the right magneto and then
the left magneto. I had to set the altimeter to the right
elevation. I had to set the transponder to the proper fre-
quency. I had to get a clear route that I would travel to
my destination.

When I did the preflight inspection, I would make sure
that there was adequate oil in the engine. I would visually
inspect to see if we had adequate gasoline. I would drain
the sump to ensure there was no water in the gas. I would
check the tires to make sure there was no cut and that the
tires were properly inflated. I would be sure that the cover
was taken off the pitot tubes to make sure that I had the
proper outside speed. I made sure the chocks were taken
off the wheels and there was no obstruction in the way.
As I gained more experience, these checks became second
nature. However, on one trip, because I had not practiced,
I forgot that the elevation of our destination was 460 feet
above sea level, whereas I had taken off about 20 feet above
sea level. Regrettably the ground came up much too fast,
because I was gearing an altimeter at sea level. This lack of
experience could have caused a serious wreck.

THE EXPONENTIAL CURVE

Why have I shared the stories about my heart surgeon and my experience as a pilot? To illustrate that the more we use what we have, the better ability we will have to use it. "Unto him who has, more will be given. And what he does not have will be taken away from him."[14] This law is inexorable and applies to individuals, to corporations, to universities, and to governments.

But as I studied the laws of the kingdom of God, I realized there was something else available to be coupled with the Law of Use—and that is called the exponential curve.

If added to the endeavor, there is a percentage increase, and the results can be staggering. Businesses are judged by four capital letters, CAGR, which stands for compound annual growth rate. Corporations that are stagnant and not growing are not highly regarded by the investment community. However, those that have a steady growth pattern are rewarded, because the investment community understands what the exponential curve can accomplish. The law of compound interest has been called the eighth wonder of the world—even Albert Einstein acknowledged its power.[15]

It seems like a joke, but it is said that if the thirty pieces of silver that Judas Iscariot used to betray Jesus were invested at a 4 percent annual compound interest rate, tax-free, by 1950 there would have been enough money to give $300,000 to every man, woman, and child on the planet.

Money invested at compound interest will double, according to the rule of 72. So, if money is invested at 20 percent compounded, it will double in just under four years. If it's invested at 10 percent compounded, it will double in approximately seven years. The thing is, the doubling continues and continues and continues, with staggering results in the long term.

For example, consider a $100 bill. If allowed to double on an exponential curve...

In one year, it is $200.

And the next year, it is $400.

The next year, it is $800.

The next year, it is $1,600.

The next year, it is $3,200.

The next year, it is $6,400.

The next year, it is $12,800.

The next year, it is $25,600.

The next year, it is $51,200.

The next year, it is $102,400.

The next year, it is $204,800.

The next year, it is $409,600.

The next year, it is $819,200.

The next year, it is $1,638,400.

At the end of twenty years, it is $104,857,600.

In five more years, it will be $3,355,443,200.

This exercise just demonstrates the enormous power of compound interest and what can happen with one lowly little $100 bill if that amount is allowed to double just in the short span of twenty-five years. Of course, we must recognize the truth of the saying that "trees do not grow to the sky." Obviously this type of compounding is not possible. But I use this example to show the incredible power of compounding.

However, a few years ago, when the prime rate was in excess of 11 percent, I found an investment that was as close to foolproof as anything I had ever seen. In those days the firms that were handling the United States' debt had created two classes of securities. One was based on the interest being charged for the debt; the other was based on the principal. The latter was sold as zero-coupon bonds, which would allow it to compound until the maturity of the instrument.

For example, a $100 bond that matured in ten years might sell on the market for as low as $20, and then at the end of ten years could be redeemed by the government or sold on the market for the face value of $100. In today's world few investments are called risk-free; however, in a high interest–rate environment, United States guaranteed zero-coupon bonds were as close to a sure thing as I have ever come across. These anomalies do appear from time to time, and the alert investor will take advantage of them. But my advice is to gain wisdom in investing and to make investment decisions with all deliberate care.

The Law of Use and the exponential curve not only apply to money, but they also apply to any activity, membership, salvation, church growth, political party, nation, and world population. The secret is to let the Law of Use and the exponential curve work in your favor.

The leading investor in the United States is a man from Omaha named Warren Buffett. Buffett's entire investment

strategy involves seeking companies that have double-digit
compound growth. Applying the Law of Use has made
him one of the richest men in America and the acknowledged expert in high finance.

If a person begins young and compounds savings at just
8 percent a year, the results can be staggering. At the same
time, a nation that violates these laws can find itself in
serious trouble. As a nation, the United States has violated
the Law of Use and the exponential curve, and our bor-
rowing and debt exceed comprehension.

In the mid-1960s, Lyndon Johnson said that he would
not be the first United States president to preside over a
$100 billion budget. Because of our profligate spending,
our nation has amassed a stated and hidden debt load
approaching $60 or $70 trillion.[16] In the year that I am
writing this, our federal deficit is approaching $1 trillion.[17]
If normal interest rates were applied to our debt, there
would be no money available for the hundreds of federal
programs the American people rely on for their well-being.
Congress has looted the so-called Social Security Trust
Fund. There is no money in this trust fund, only federal
IOUs.[18] We are told that the Medicare Trust Fund will be
depleted within a short span of years. And whether we like
it or not, we as a nation and we as citizens of the world are
facing a fiscal collapse of epic proportions that will destroy
the way of life we have all enjoyed.

GROWTH OR STAGNATION

Let's bring the Law of Use closer to home. A few years ago I was riding on a commercial flight when the flight attendant, who knew who I was, sat down next to me and began to ask my advice. She was a stunningly beautiful black woman, tall, athletic looking, and very intelligent. In her job she had traveled widely and had learned about the world. She was well educated and well read. She clearly had been exercising the Law of Use in her life, and everything about her showed accomplishment. But her story was very sad.

Some years before, she had fallen in love with a man who was her peer in ability. But over the years, he had let himself go. He was fat and slovenly. He did not care for his physical appearance, and he did not attempt to further his learning. He was stuck in what would be called a time warp. My flight attendant friend did not want to leave her husband, but every day their life together became intolerable for her. What should she do?

She could pray for him. She could love him. She could hope that friends would inspire him to seek a more disciplined life. But unless something was done, their marriage was heading for a shipwreck, because the wife's life reflected growth through the Law of Use and the husband's life represented stagnation.

I am aware of an even more dramatic example. A dear friend of mine was employed in an automobile factory at a wage of some eight dollars an hour forty to fifty years ago. He had married his high school sweetheart.

She was beautiful, vivacious, and the love of his life. He was humble. She was humble. They loved each other very much and foresaw a life together. Then something began to happen.

The husband left his factory job, bought a couple of used cars, and opened a used car lot. He was a born salesman and soon began selling many used cars. As he gained more money, he sought out an underrepresented national car company and obtained a franchise to sell that brand in his hometown. In order to succeed, he had to learn property management, bookkeeping, finance terms, and automobile maintenance.

Soon he decided that he could sell more cars if he was on television, so he negotiated a morning spot on a local television station. Along with that came instruction as to lighting, makeup, and dialogue. As the years went by, he was selling more cars than anyone in the state and became the friend of the executives of one or more major automobile corporations. As he won awards, he was given trips to exotic vacation spots, where he mingled with the cream of automobile society.

But what about his beautiful high school sweetheart? She took no courses and did not learn anything about business. She learned nothing about fashion or the decorative arts that wealthy people have in their homes. She did not try to gain the necessary social skills to converse intelligently with people who were not high school graduates or factory workers. A tragedy of the first order was developing. The Law of Use had propelled her husband higher and higher. When this happened, bitterness came into the marriage, along with jealousy and resentment.

The husband, at the beginning of the marriage, had a partner that he could love and with whom he could communicate. Fifteen years down the road, he wanted a partner who could share his achievements, but his sweet, loving wife wasn't up to the task. That marriage headed inexorably toward the divorce court.

I make this challenge now: Realize that life is not static. We either grow or we die. And to both wives and husbands I give this advice: Always seek growth, seek knowledge, have broad interests, take extra courses, read extensively, expand your circle of friends, and use to the fullest whatever you have. Without being obtrusive, learn what you can about your spouse's activities so that you will be an equal partner in a marriage that grows and flourishes throughout the years.

When your spouse succeeds, always rejoice in his or her accomplishments. To men the Bible says, "Delight in the wife of your youth."[19] Always keep the spark of love alive.

In God's kingdom there is no end to learning, to spiritual growth, or to the love of God in your life. The Bible says, "Love is of God; and everyone who loves is born of God and knows God."[20] The Bible tells us that "a merry heart does good, like medicine, but a broken spirit dries the bones."[21] God intends couples to grow in love for each other until the day they pass off the scene. One important admonition is to leave rancor alone at bedtime and to practice the presence of God and to practice love. Each day think of at least ten things that you admire about your spouse, and then repeat them over and over again until you're established in love for one another.

Chapter 2

THE LAW OF RECIPROCITY

THE LAW OF Use is the fundamental principle of growth and development for human beings and for whatever organization human beings are associated with. In the interaction between human beings, between organizations, and between people and God Almighty, there is the Law of Reciprocity.

I have a story to illustrate how that works.

During one of my college summers, I took a job with the United States Forest Service to work on a crew that was on hand to fight forest fires. I was assigned to a ranger station in the Lolo National Forest on the border of Idaho some miles west of Missoula, Montana. I lived in a bunkhouse on the second floor of the ranger station, along with a team of fellows assigned to clean debris from the forest in an operation called slash disposal.

One day, however, my duties were somewhat different. The officials wanted the telephone lines cleared along the high ridges between lookout points. I was driven with one of the senior young men to a dirt trail on top of a mountain and told to walk along the ridge, repairing telephone lines. I was given a climbing belt and a set of climbing spurs so that I could climb up telephone poles to fix wires where it was necessary. I also was given a crosscut saw that I carried on my back to take care of trees or branches that had fallen across the lines. I set out on a hot July day, climbing telephone poles and sawing logs in the hot sun.

I was quite thirsty by noon, and I asked the senior fellow who was with me if I could use his canteen to get a drink. He smiled broadly and told me that he didn't think we would need one and he had neglected to bring any water. I was climbing, walking, and sawing under a blazing hot sun high in the Rocky Mountains, and my thirst became more intense every minute.

Finally we reached the end of the ridge and were able to walk down into the valley where there was a stream of water. I dropped the crosscut saw from my shoulder and ran like one of the figures you may have seen in a motion picture to get at the water. I threw myself down on the bank and began to drink heartily of the cold liquid. After I had quenched my thirst, I looked up, and lo and behold, about two hundred yards upstream was a small herd of cattle standing in the water and dropping the waste that cattle always drop in that situation. Fortunately I wasn't diseased from drinking the water, but undoubtedly it had gotten polluted without my knowing it. You might ask, "What has the image of cattle muddying the stream got to do with the Law of Reciprocity?" I'll share something much more spiritual.

THE GOLDEN RULE

By the mid-1960s our broadcast in Virginia Beach had resulted in a wonderful move of the Holy Spirit of God. People by the thousands had received Christ, the joy of the Lord was in people's lives, and there was love between us and our audiences. We were drinking from clear, cool water, and the joy that we had was not tarnished by carnality, greed, or suspicion. Then into that clear stream stepped several individuals who stomped around and muddied the water. Their conduct introduced suspicion and public opprobrium on those who were religious broadcasters. Instead of people who were honestly proclaiming the gospel for the good of the audience, religious broadcasters were labeled television evangelists. And in the public mind the term *television evangelist* soon became synonymous with *sleazy crook*. Streams that are muddied will ultimately cleanse themselves, but in this case it has taken decades to remove the pollution that was brought into a clear, beautiful stream of water by a few self-serving individuals.

What is called the Golden Rule—"Do unto others as you would have them do unto you"—has been stated not only by Jesus but also by other religious thinkers. In this case, if you wouldn't want somebody muddying your clear spring, don't muddy someone else's clear spring. But how else does this simple principle apply to the interpersonal relations that we all enjoy?

Communities have established rigid zoning laws to force people to follow the Golden Rule. It's simple. If you wouldn't want someone to build an ugly shack in your neighborhood of fine homes, don't build one in theirs. If you don't want a fire hazard next to your house, then don't put a fire hazard next to someone else's house. If you wouldn't want a neighbor to have a dog barking loudly all night long next to your house, then don't allow your dog to bark loudly all night long next to the neighbor's house. As a matter of fact, the acronym NIMBY is often used to describe this phenomenon. It stands for "not in my backyard."

Around the turn of the twentieth century an entrepreneur named William Love decided that if he could connect the upper and lower Niagara Rivers through a canal, the resulting force could fuel hydroelectric power for significant parts of upstate New York. Unfortunately, before his dream could be realized, the nation had turned to the power grid that had been proposed by the Italian genius Nikola Tesla; therefore, hydroelectric power was not needed in upstate New York because adequate electric power was available more cheaply.[1] However, a portion of the Love Canal had already been built. So what use could it have?

In the 1920s the State of New York designated the Love Canal as a repository for harmful chemicals. The Hooker Chemical Company began storing barrels of their chemicals in this big ditch. As the years went by, the ditch was covered over with dirt, and it appeared the dangerous chemicals had been satisfactorily disposed of. Hooker sold the site for $1, and the city planned a lovely neighborhood on the property.[2]

For about twenty years the community of one hundred homes and a school appeared to thrive. Then in August 1978, reports of a nightmare began to surface—literally.

Over the years, heavy rain seeped through the topsoil and caused the barrels of chemicals to expand and explode. Then people who had bought or built homes over this landfill experienced severe cancers, and they began having children with birth defects. The ground in certain parts began to expand, and one swimming pool actually popped out of the ground.[3]

The suffering caused by this tragedy was unimaginable. Finally the state and federal government were forced to step in, relocate the families, and try as best they could to remediate the problem.

We ask ourselves who caused this problem and who violated the Law of Reciprocity. Certainly it wasn't William Love. Was it the city? Was it the Hooker Chemical Company? Was it the developers who sold the lots near Love Canal? Perhaps the finger of blame should be pointed at the city officials who eagerly accepted the land and then permitted innocent homeowners to live on it. Surely experts must have realized that a toxic wasteland lurked beneath this neighborhood. No one should have been allowed to live there. But someone had failed the Law of Reciprocity.

At present our nation is experiencing what is called an opioid crisis. It began as Purdue Pharma and other chemical companies discovered a substance that was probably one hundred times more powerful than morphine.[4]

Dr. Richard Sackler began a one-man crusade to convince doctors that they should exercise all of their skills to keep their patients from experiencing pain caused

by cancer or surgery or arthritis or some type of indus-
trial accident. The manufactured painkiller was called
OxyContin®, a timed-release formula of the powerful anal-
gesic oxycodone. The officials of these chemical companies
did not consider that the painkillers they were creating
had become highly addictive. Yes, they did alleviate pain,
but yes, they were also addictive. Yet more than that, they
were enormously profitable.

The Sackler family became multibillionaires, and the
corporations making these painkillers amassed enormous profits.[5] Doctors who prescribed the painkillers
helped create a steady stream of dependent patients, and
their incomes soared. The statistics of how many tablets
of OxyContin® and oxycodone were sold in small rural
communities in states like West Virginia and Ohio and
up and down the east coast of Florida are absolutely staggering. Although it was clear that these manufactured
painkillers became addictive after three days of doses,[6]
the pharmaceutical companies lobbied their congressmen
to include a label with these drugs that they were safe for
continued use.

From my reading on the subject, I have learned that
withdrawal from these opioids is virtually impossible
without some intermediate letdown period. Otherwise, the
user is condemned to a virtual hell on earth. As a result,
this quite often leads to a mental institution or to suicide.

Imagine what the difference would have been in our
society if those involved in the manufacture, sale, and

prescription of opioids had just put in place the Golden Rule: "Do unto others as you would have them do unto you."

There are at least fifty thousand deaths every year on the highways of the United States, not to mention the tens of thousands of people who are permanently maimed because of highway injuries. Driving a high-powered auto-mobile at a high rate of speed is very exhilarating, to be sure. But the cost of lives and suffering from this pleasure is beyond calculation. Again, if we would not like for a reckless or drunk driver to kill one of our children, let's be sure that while driving we are not reckless or inattentive or mentally impaired and take the life of someone else's child by our conduct. Again, the Golden Rule would save so much suffering and so much cost for the police to patrol our highways. "Do unto others as you would have them do unto you."

I was just a youngster when World War II began, but I think of the terrible suffering that was caused by the madness of a dictator like Adolf Hitler or the aggressions of warlords who tried to ease punitive sanctions placed upon them by the United States by destroying our fleet in the Pacific. Approximately fifty million people died during World War II, and those deaths could have been avoided by the simple application of the Golden Rule.

The time will come when the Lord Jesus Christ will rule the nations of the earth, and the Word that God has spoken to us will be in effect to bring peace among all nations. We are told that humanity will live in peace and will no longer study for war. Think what that would mean if the nearly $700 billion a year that we spend on our military were diverted to civilian activities—to schools, to music, to art, to medicine. We could begin to see a true millennium if our resources and energies were no longer devoted to killing or defense against killing.

AN EQUAL AND OPPOSITE REACTION

One of the key physical principles underlying the Law of Reciprocity is simple: "For every action, there is an equal and opposite reaction."

I once told a paternal uncle how nice people were in an area into which I had just moved. My uncle wisely said, "Pat, you will find people are always nice when you are nice to them."

A psychologist ran a test on the streets of New York. One day, he walked down the sidewalk and scowled at people. Some of them stepped out of his way, others scowled back, and some even raised their fists and threatened him. The next day, he smiled at each passerby, who in turn responded with a smile and a cheery greeting. Jesus said this: "Give, and it will be given to you: good measure, pressed down, shaken together, and running over will be put into your bosom."[7]

People must realize that Jesus is giving us the key to open heaven's bounty. I repeat what He said: "Give and it will be given unto you; pressed down, good measure will then be heaped into your bosom." How many descriptions—*pressed down, good measure, heaped*—should He add to get our attention? Look at the trees during autumn when seeds begin to fall. It's not just one or two; it's hundreds of thousands that fall to the ground. When we give to the Lord's work, the return is not just double or triple. It is thirty, sixty, or one hundred times as much as we give. We are told that giving leads to abundance and that withholding gifts leads to poverty. God will be no one's debtor, and if we give, He will repay liberally.

One technique that I have used puts the Law of Reciprocity to work in a magnificent way. I call it "anticipatory tithing." What sum would I anticipate receiving? If it's $1,000, I would give $100. If it's $10,000, I would give $1,000. If it's $100,000, I would give $10,000. I would do violence to the majesty of the Lord and to our walk as Christians if I even suggested that the kingdom of heaven was like some heavenly slot machine. But I do feel strongly that we can base our finances on the express Word of the Son of God. We don't give to get, but we give because we love Him and desire to help those in need.

Nevertheless we can give with the full assurance that what we give to the work of God here on earth will bring forth bounty from heaven—which, over the years, will amaze us.

We are also told that it is a sin to tempt the Lord our God. As a matter of fact, Jesus clearly spoke to Satan in just this fashion when He was being tempted and refused to endanger His own life to force God to save Him. Nevertheless in the Book of the prophet Malachi (Malachi means my messenger) we are told, "'And try Me now in this,' says the LORD of hosts, 'if I will not open for you the windows of heaven and pour out for you such blessing that there will not be room enough to receive it.'"[8] It obviously is no sin to give generously to God's work and expect that the God who made the promise in Malachi will "open for you the windows of heaven and pour out for you such blessing that there will not be room enough to receive it."[9]

The most important teaching today about business is customer service. If businesses serve their customers, their customers will serve them with loyalty and repeat business. If a business cheats the customer, that customer may well be gone forever. I once read that the people who take customer service calls should be given lavish quarters and made to feel comfortable so that they can project that feeling to those who call. Again, if we would not want some abusive, ill-tempered individual on the phone talking to us, why would we have an ill-tempered, ill-informed person speaking to others? It's so simple and it is so profound. "Do unto others as you would have them do unto you."

At the end of World War II, the Nazis learned the principle of jet propulsion. As a thrust went from the exhaust of a jet engine, the jet airplane was thrust forward. A brilliant scientist named Wernher von Braun perfected jet propulsion at a secret center called Peenemünde.[10] Up to that time, the Nazis could deliver bombs over London using aircraft. However, the Luftwaffe had been driven out of the skies by the Royal Air Force (RAF). Von Braun, using the principle of jet propulsion, developed what was called a V-2 rocket that could be launched from continental Europe into British cities without the need for a pilot. Von Braun was also developing jet aircraft that could fly much faster than propeller planes using the principle of jet propulsion, based on Newton's third law of motion—"For every action, there is an equal and opposite reaction." Had the Nazi regime not fallen apart when it did, there is a real possibility that the Germans could have developed jet airplanes that could have taken the RAF out of the skies.

In our modern era, after World War II, NASA recruited von Braun and others of his associates from Germany and moved on to the massive rocket programs with which we are all familiar. The scientists developed the mathematical formula for determining the velocity that was needed in a rocket to escape the gravitational pull of earth. Giant rockets were then assembled in places like Cape Canaveral in Florida to launch vehicles into orbit around the earth— and ultimately to take a crew of astronauts out of earth's gravitational field all the way to a landing on the moon.

But how does this law work in terms of interpersonal relations? The Bible says, "A soft answer turns away wrath, but a harsh word stirs up anger."[11] It's very simple. If a door with a hinge is pushed open violently, it will snap back with equal violence. An action that is begun with violence will snap back with equal violence. That's why in the secret kingdom, the kingdom of God, wise people will use gentleness when dealing with others.

Here is an example from my horse-riding days. One day I was riding my big Lusitano horse, Ufano. I gave him a signal for a canter, and he didn't move. I repeated the signal, and again he did not move. The third time, I spurred him on, and instead of cantering forward, he began to canter backward. Many riders, upon that act of disobedience, would have beat the horse with a whip. Instead I tried to determine what was wrong. My solution was simple. Another rider had been working Ufano on a regular basis and had given a cue that was different from mine. I sent word to this individual that I had bought Ufano to ride, not to make him available for her to train. Within a short period of time Ufano and I were working as a team, and he willingly followed my cues as we moved into higher levels of what is called dressage. Had I exercised harsh discipline over him because he misunderstood my cue, I would have created a surly animal that did not trust me as his leader.

In dealing with another human being, especially a spouse or a child, harsh accusation will always bring forth an angry response. I am a firm believer in blaming myself if a problem arises, or at least asking the other person what caused the problem. Imagine the reaction of a spouse who is told by his or her partner that he or she takes the blame for whatever was done. Not only would a conflict be avoided, but the guilty party would also do everything possible to take responsibility for the action. And the result would be harmony instead of strife.

Think what would happen not only in domestic situations but also in all manner of labor relations if management would attempt to understand the feelings of the workers—and then would attempt to alleviate problems instead of offering harsh criticism and blame. Without question, human beings are always more creative when they can think freely instead of cringing under the lash of harsh criticism and blame. I have no conception of how much animosity has been engendered by bosses who take credit for the creative work of their subordinates and who blame them for mistakes that they themselves have made in the course of business.

HOLDING OURSELVES ACCOUNTABLE

A long time ago, I set as a goal for myself to give God the credit for all the good things that were done. It was His wisdom, His power, His direction, His work...and all the credit went to Him. On the other hand, I would take the blame for all the mistakes that were made. If there was a foul-up in an operation, it was my fault, not God's.

The Bible tells us that the sinners in the days of John the Baptist "justified God, having been baptized with the baptism of John."[12]

I am simply amazed that natural disasters would be described as "acts of God"—tragedies, like famine and disease, would be described as acts of God. Yet it is clear that God set in motion the laws of cause and effect. And so much of what happens in our lives is not God's fault; it is ours. I was amazed recently to read the statement of an openly gay candidate for the 2020 presidential election. In discussing his gay marriage of two years, he said, "If you got a problem with who I am, your problem is not with me. Your quarrel...is with my creator."[13]

So many are willing to blame God for their own failings. Many in our population are morbidly obese, yet any attempt to help them is considered "hateful." A young child is unable to identify his gender, and we allow physical mutilation as part of his gender identity; yet we castigate a leading pediatric neurosurgeon who speaks against such practices as promoting hate speech. A noted astrophysicist recently told me that the God we serve is a trillion trillion times smarter than we are, yet we think He does not understand our modern processes or the way we live or the way we behave.

If we hold ourselves accountable, then we will work to improve ourselves and correct things that are wrong. The God we serve cannot make mistakes—because He is all-wise and all-knowing. So how could any mere mortal claim that God didn't know what He was doing and that mistakes in marriage, finances, and business were somehow God's fault? The blessing of God will come upon someone who acknowledges and forsakes his or her sin. Such a person will receive rich blessings rather than condemnation.

CHAPTER 3

THE LAW OF RESPONSIBILITY

I N THE SECRET kingdom of God, all of us are measured by a principle set forth by Jesus Christ. "To whom much is given, from him much will be required."[1] Think about how this works.

If someone said to me, "Build an automobile," I would laugh, and then, working as hard as possible, I might be able to create one fender. If a machine shop was told to build an automobile, after a year they might create one crudely built vehicle and feel they'd succeeded. However, if General Motors was told to build an automobile and all they created was one, they would have failed miserably, because the expectation would be that with the factories, the finances, and the expertise available to them, their output would be in the millions of cars, not one or two.

Here's another example. If a small mom-and-pop business was asked to make a profit and they achieved $10,000 in revenue, they would be commended for their skill and diligence. If Chase Manhattan Bank had an annual profit of $10,000, their chairman would be fired, and investors would desert them in droves because they have available resources capable of deriving billions of dollars of profit on an annual basis, not a few thousand.

To put it in a spiritual context, if a small church of a thousand members brought a hundred people to faith in

Jesus Christ in a year, they would be commended for their diligence. If CBN, which broadcasts in over 80 languages in over 150 countries and territories, won 100 people to faith in Jesus in a year, it would be considered a dreadful failure. "To whom much is given, much will be required." Whether it's in business, in finance, in spiritual ministry, in education, in art, in music—wherever we have found ourselves—the secret kingdom demands that we bring forth a return from our life's work that is commensurate with the opportunities placed in our hands.

This kingdom law certainly keeps pride in check. Jesus told His disciples, "When you have done all those things which you are commanded, say, 'We are unprofitable servants. We have done what was our duty to do.'"[2]

When I began The Christian Broadcasting Network, I had $70, a used DeSoto car, a few pots and pans, and some baby beds. My first bank account was opened with three $1 bills. As I used what was given me, it began to grow. And with the exponential curve, at the end of twenty years our annual income was $50 million. In the early days, if I had been able to lead four or five people to faith, it would have been a significant accomplishment. As I write these words, our surveys indicate that our programs have resulted in over one hundred million people around the world coming to faith. How could we possibly rest secure if we failed to live up to what's been placed in our hands? "Unto him who has been given much, much will be required." The more we receive and the more we learn and the more skills we achieve, the higher the demands will be on our lives.

I am interested in the way the Old Testament describes the death of certain kings. It is said that the king "rested with his ancestors."[3] So much is said today about preparing for retirement. People want retirement to begin at sixty-five or maybe sixty-six or sixty-seven. In the Bible there was no retirement. People lived and served God and became His witnesses on earth and continued to work. Then the Bible says, "They rested with their ancestors."

I once received a question on my television show, *The 700 Club*, in which the viewer stated, "After I die, I thought I could take it easy and lie out on the beach for all eternity." I thought that was one of the most ridiculous things I had ever heard, because I personally hate the thought of being idle.

In truth, the apostle Paul says that the saints will judge the angels.[4] That task is enough to keep us all busy. But according to Regent University's visiting professor, astrophysicist Dr. Hugh Ross, there are a billion trillion stars the size of our sun in the universe, and in the world to come, if God wants to, He will have no problem assigning a planet to each of His saints to manage for all eternity. "To whom much is given, much will be required."

CHAPTER 4

THE LAW OF GREATNESS

AROUND THREE HUNDRED years before the birth of Christ, Alexander, the son of Philip II of Macedonia, entered the world stage. He succeeded his father, and after consolidating his power among the Greek states, he took an army of Macedonian warriors into Persia. He was a brilliant general who, after successive victories, gained control of the former Persian and Babylonian empires and stopped his incredible advance only at the Indus River in what we now know as India. He has been called Alexander the Great, but was he truly great? He died at age thirty-three after spending months in wild debauchery. It is said he wept because he had no more worlds to conquer. After his death his empire was divided into four parts, headed by his leading generals. He was called "great," but after his tragic end, can it truly be said that he was great?

In Russia, a leader named Peter the Great emerged who attempted to unify his nation. To enable it to compete with European powers, Peter actually went undercover and taught himself the craft of shipbuilding so that he could instruct his nobles in this art. Peter died at age fifty-two of gangrene caused by a failed operation on his infected bladder. Was he truly "great" or just another failed human being?

In our modern day, a boxer whose given name was Cassius Clay later took on the name Muhammad Ali. He loudly proclaimed in his heyday that he was "the greatest." As good a boxer as he was, he still suffered from a type of dementia and the resulting tremors. Despite his protestations, was Muhammad Ali truly great?

A SERVANT OF ALL

We are told in the Bible that as Jesus and His disciples were traveling on the road to Jerusalem in what would become the prelude to His crucifixion, James and John asked if they could sit at Jesus' right and left hand. Jesus' other disciples were displeased about the request. Jesus knew what was causing the dissension and said: "You know that those who are considered rulers over the Gentiles lord it over them, and their great ones exercise authority over them. Yet it shall not be so among you; but whoever desires to become great among you shall be your servant. And whoever of you desires to be first shall be slave [servant] of all."[1] Doesn't this teaching absolutely fly in the face of our expectations?

In the common parlance, a great man would be able to order people around and have large enterprises under his control. To the carnal man, being a servant lacks appeal. But consider the incredible scope of this teaching of the kingdom. If we were to name the ten greatest people of the past centuries, we would invariably list some of those who served the most: Mother Teresa of Calcutta; Albert Schweitzer, who served the poor and needy in Lambaréné in Gabon; Thomas Edison, who brought the miracle of electric lighting to billions of people; and J. C. Penney, who served millions of people with low-cost merchandise. But of course the greatest of all was Jesus Christ Himself, who died to bring life and hope to billions of people throughout the world.

We are told that on the night before His crucifixion, during the Passover meal with His disciples, Jesus laid aside His robe, took a pan of water and a towel, and performed the function of a slave by washing His disciples' feet. He said to them, "You call Me Teacher and Lord, and you say well, for so I am. If I then, your Lord and Teacher, have washed your feet, you also ought to wash one another's feet."[2] The greatest of all took on the role of a slave. The Bible says that He did not consider equality with God a thing to be grasped but took on the form of a servant made conformable to death on the cross.[3] In practical terms today, the key to success is giving service—the better the service, the greater the reward.

After serving in World War II, a young man named Sam Walton managed a little store in Bentonville, Arkansas. His goal was to serve his customers with the lowest prices possible. He then brought in IBM to devise methods of simplifying his supply chain.[4] Without ceasing, Sam Walton found ways to cut costs and provide a service of lower prices to those who shopped at his store. It wasn't long before his one store was so successful that he opened others. Over the decades Walmart stores became the model of retail efficiency, and collectively, Sam Walton's heirs became the wealthiest family in America—all because of a slavish adherence to the Law of Greatness: "Let him who is great among you be the servant of all."

Each of us must determine if we truly are servants. Schools should serve their children, coaches should serve their teams, brokers should serve their clients, lawyers and doctors and other professional people should serve their patients and clients. A dear friend of mine recently passed away. Before he died, he had established the largest medical practice in the state of Ohio. Why? The answer is simple. He served his patients with diligence, patience, and loving care.

If you wish to be great, don't try to do it by lording over your subordinates, but spend your time thinking of ways you can serve them—make them happier, make their lives easier, provide ways that you can simplify their tasks.

Perhaps the greatest coach in all history was John Wooden, the legendary coach of UCLA basketball. Time and again he turned out championship teams, and players he coached went on to become stars in professional basketball. Wooden considered himself first of all a Christian and a servant to the teams he coached. No matter was too small for his attention. He made sure his players learned how to put their socks on right so that their feet did not blister.[5] He taught them the fundamentals of ballhandling. Over and over again he led them through simple drills until they became the best they could be. Because their leader was a servant, the UCLA basketball teams won an incredible ten championships in twelve seasons, including a record seven in a row. Let him who is great among you be the servant of all.[6]

CHAPTER 5

THE LAW OF MIRACLES

NOT ONLY IS the secret kingdom the law for us to follow to be blessed on this earth, but it is also a guide to the miraculous. In Mark 11 we have an exchange between Jesus and His disciples. In it is the formula for the miraculous in our lives.

According to the story, as Jesus and His disciples were leaving Bethany and Jesus was hungry, He saw a fig tree in full leaf and went to it seeking a couple of figs to satisfy His appetite. He reached up and found that its fruitfulness was an illusion.[1] As we continue the story, we find that it is clear that the fig tree stood for Israel, which, with its magnificent ceremonies and richly garbed priests, was holding out to worshippers the promise of salvation. When the worshippers reached for true spiritual nourishment, they came up with disappointment and disillusionment. In fact, they were even cheated of their money by money changers that were outside the door of the temple, because only temple currency was allowed as offerings by the worshippers.

Nevertheless Jesus looked at the fig tree and said, "Let no one eat fruit from you ever again."[2] They passed by the fig tree, descended the Mount of Olives, and then entered the temple grounds in Jerusalem. That evening they returned to Bethany to spend the night, and on the next morning, they headed from Bethany back to Jerusalem. On the way, they passed by the little fig tree, and to the amazement of the disciples, the little tree had withered from the roots.

Peter shouted in amazement, "Rabbi, look! The fig tree which You cursed has withered away."[3] Obviously Peter wasn't wasting his breath saying something that was evident to all of them. What he was essentially saying was, "Lord, how did You do it? Tell us the secret of such a wonderful miracle." Jesus replied, "Have faith in God."[4] This is the key to all miracles. "Without faith it is impossible to please Him, for he who comes to God must believe that He is, and that He is a rewarder of those who diligently seek Him."[5]

The Bible tells us that "faith is the substance of things hoped for, the evidence of things not seen."[6] It also tells us that a double-minded man can receive nothing from the Lord.[7] If a person is to receive a miracle, he or she must be absolutely convinced of the power of God, of the goodness of God, and of the ability of God to do what He promised.

FAITH AND DOUBT

In the fourth chapter of Romans we hear of Abraham, who was one hundred years old, and his wife, Sarah, who was ninety years old. Together they had no child, yet they had been promised a child by almighty God. Despite the deadness of his body and the deadness of her womb, Abraham believed the promise that God had given him. We read the wonderful statement that Abraham "was strengthened in faith, giving glory to God, and being fully convinced that what He had promised He was also able to perform."[8] If there is to be a miracle, we must be fully persuaded that God is able to perform what He has promised. The double-minded man will receive nothing from the Lord.

We read in the Bible that the universe as we know it—the earth and the other planets, the natural laws, the vegetation, the animals, the birds, and human beings—all came into being because of the word of God. God did not pray that this would happen; He declared it to be. So also, when we look for miracles in the kingdom, we speak the Word. The Bible tells us, "A man shall eat well by the fruit of his mouth."[9] So, with faith in God, the next step is a declaration of what we want to accomplish. Jesus said to the fig tree, "Let no one eat fruit from you ever again."[10] It was a curse, and it came to pass exactly as it was spoken. So, He told His disciples, with faith in God, if they spoke to the mountain and told it to be cast into the sea, it would obey them.[11] If you stand on the Mount of Olives, it's possible to look down far below into the Dead Sea, so Jesus was telling His disciples that a bold declaration under the anointing of God would have actually caused the Mount of Olives to tumble down and fall into the Dead Sea. But the caution quickly followed: "and does not doubt in his heart."[12]

There are actually two types of faith described in the Bible. One is the faith that is a fruit of the Spirit and grows, like love and joy, as the heart learns more about the heavenly Father and faith in Him grows. There is another faith that is a supernatural gift. This is a sudden infusion of heavenly faith that causes mountains to move, the Dead Sea to part, and the dead to be raised. If someone declares, "I believe it wasn't going to happen anyhow," he or she has already indicated the doubt that would not bring forth miracles.

Another great faith killer is the phrase that seems so spiritual: "If it be thy will." If it's not His will, we shouldn't be asking for it. It's important to seek what God wants first and to learn His will—and then, without any doubt, to declare the deed done. Miracle prayer does not include the phrase "if it be thy will."

So, let's review. We start with unquenchable faith in the God of miracles. We then declare specifically what it is we want to have done. Then we do not doubt in our hearts. And the Bible says we shall have the thing that we say.[13] All of these premises rest on the assumption that the person doing the declaring is born again. That in turn means having sins forgiven, and for that to happen, we must remember the Lord's Prayer, which says, "Forgive us our debts, as we forgive our debtors."[14] So, we now have this cardinal admonition from our Lord: "Whenever you stand praying, if you have anything against anyone, forgive him, that your Father in heaven may also forgive you your trespasses."[15] If a person harbors bitterness toward another, is filled with resentment, is unwilling to forgive a slight that has taken place, either by a spouse or a parent or a child or an employer or a fellow employee or a friend or an enemy, there needs to be forgiveness. This is the absolute sine qua non to miracles.

Without a forgiving heart there will be no miracle. But in the kingdom of God normal Christianity will mean a life of miracles, of supernatural blessing, of ongoing answers to prayer, and of fellowship with the heavenly Father. Why would anyone settle for less?

CHAPTER 6

THE LAW OF UNITY

WE LEARN IN the Bible that in the early days of humanity, the few people in existence began to rebel against their Creator. In an act of defiance they decided to unite their efforts and build a tall tower that would reach into heaven and permit them to challenge the God of heaven.

We are told in the Bible that God came down to look at this rebellious endeavor, and then He made a startling pronouncement: "Now the whole earth had one language and a common speech....If as one people speaking the same language they have begun to do this, then nothing they plan to do will be impossible for them."[1] Can you imagine what this means? The God of the universe is saying that even rebellious people who act in unity can perform impossible tasks. And if this is the case for rebels, how much more could be accomplished by men and women who seek to serve God's will in unity?

On the reverse side of this, Jesus made it clear that a house divided against itself could not stand, nor could a kingdom divided against itself stand.[2] The surest way to destroy a nation is to set its people against one another.

The noted anarchist Saul Alinsky set forth a series of principles on how to undermine a nation, and foremost in his teaching was the concept of dissatisfaction and disunity.

If he could turn workers against management, customers against businesses, men against women, citizens against their leaders, he could guarantee the collapse of the society.

But think of the wonderful things a nation can do when a people unite together. We can build railroads across a wilderness. We can erect beautiful skyscrapers. We can pave hundreds of miles of interstate highways. We can create just laws that are the wonder of the world. And of course we could follow the challenge of a president that we could build a rocket to carry passengers to the moon and then bring them home again.

THE POWER OF WORKING IN HARMONY

I have an example that is closer to home. In the early days of CBN the Lord instructed me to "build a school for His glory." I started with seven professors and seventy-seven students in a rented office building. And year after year, with the Law of Use, this small school began to grow.

When we had about 350 students, it was apparent to me that we needed an adequate library and classrooms to accommodate 1,000 students. If we failed to do that, the school would be crushed and ultimately die. So I had an architect work with me to design a library building that had adequate classrooms to accommodate 1,000 students. We lacked the money to pay for such a structure, but I had enough funds available to set out the dimensions of the proposed building and to pour sand for its footing. I asked the trustees of the university to join hands with me and pray for God to bring forth the building upon whose footings we then stood. The board was in complete unity that this structure would be built according to the plans that they had approved.

At that point it was clear to me that our chief financial officer at CBN, who was a former New York banker, felt we did not have the funds available to undertake the $12 million building program. He called various groups together and gave them one message: "This university project is folly. We just can't afford to get involved in something like this at a time when we are not even paying our own bills."

I had the Word of God burning in my heart and knew His mandate to bless what was then called CBN University, so what could I do?

I called our staff together and had them sit on bleachers in our studio. I told them, "Here is the proposition. I feel that God wants us to build the library and classrooms for CBN University. If we don't, the school will die." Then I made clear to them that even if this plan was not of God, if we all were in agreement, it would succeed. On the other hand, even if it was of God and we had dissension in our ranks, the enterprise would fail. I knew that this unity was important. So, I went further and told the staff, "I'm not asking you to do any work on it. I'm not asking you to give any money toward it. I'm not asking you to be involved in any way that you don't want to. All I ask is that if you disagree, that you keep your mouth shut about it and don't stir up dissension." I said, "Is that too much to ask?" And they clearly said, "No, it isn't." And we agreed that we would all be together on this project.

I remembered the words of the Lord at the Tower of Babel: "If as one people speaking the same language they have begun to do this, then nothing they plan to do will be impossible for them."[3]

We signed the contract on faith, and the builder began to build the library and classrooms. Then the God who honors unity began to perform a miracle. The bill for the first month was $1 million. An extra million came in from unexpected sources. The second month another million appeared from unexpected sources. The third month, another million. The fourth month, another million. The fifth month, another million. And so it went, month after month, until twelve months had elapsed and $12 million had been received.

The classrooms and library were completed debt-free, the students began their studies, and what then became Regent University grew to become one of the premiere educational institutions in the nation—all because we worked together in unity.

Amazingly, over the years, as if a giant faucet would be turned on or off, as long as the staff worked in harmony with joy and love, the faucet was turned on, and bountiful finances became available for us to do our work. However, when the time came that there was dissension and bickering, the giant faucet was turned off, and funds became scarce. I know firsthand the importance of the Law of Unity.

A HOUSE DIVIDED

Today in America some 50 percent of marriages end in divorce. Husbands and wives cannot agree on how to handle their finances, on where to live, on how to discipline their children, or even on the color of their kitchen walls.

A few decades ago the leading so-called feminists asserted that they wanted to bring down the "patrimony." The tax laws mitigate against successful families. Psychiatrists urge unhappy spouses to enter into extramarital sexual affairs. Educators have tried to turn children against their parents and to break down the bond of respect that should exist between parents and children.

We learn that some time ago, the Marxist Communist plan to destroy America included overt and subtle attacks on the unity of society at all levels. The so-called progressives seem to apply biblical principles better than church people. A house divided cannot stand—a kingdom divided cannot stand—a community divided cannot stand—an enterprise divided cannot stand.

When husbands and wives love one another, when they observe the proper biblical order, when they bring up their children in the nurture and admonition of the Lord, when children respect their parents, when there is unity, there will be success. They have one mind and one voice. Now nothing they propose to do will be impossible unto them.

CHAPTER 7

THE LAW OF PERSEVERANCE

As I POINTED out, the Law of Use is the fundamental principle for human growth and development and for the growth and development of businesses, associations, political parties, and nations. However, individuals have to understand that in most cases, it is unwise to relax and expect the Law of Use to bring about dramatic results unaided.

I am thinking of a corporation called LIN Broadcasting. When LIN went public, its management decided to grant vested stock to all its employees. According to a story circulated at the time, one such employee received several thousand shares of LIN stock and quickly sold the stock to buy a small baby grand piano. Soon after this, LIN became a stock market darling, and its shares had a meteoric rise. For the employee who sold his shares to buy a piano, the market value of the stock he gave up was worth an incredible $1 million. So, he sadly looked at the piano and said, "This is a $1 million piano sitting in my living room." Had he merely persevered and held on to his stock, he could have used a small portion to buy what he wanted and could have been living comfortably on the rest.

NO TURNING BACK

For many years I have dealt with primitive nations in Africa. In one case, I tried to assist a poor village by giving them a yearling steer. I explained that if they fed and cared for the two-hundred-pound youngster, in two or three years it would grow to one thousand pounds, and then they could slaughter it and have a large quantity of beef to sell or to eat. They took my words under advisement and then came back with short-term thinking. They saw before them some steaks and roasts and hamburger. They had no intention of letting that opportunity leave, and the decision was "kill the beef, and do it now."

We are told that the Spanish conquistador Hernando Cortés made a bold decision when he reached the shores of Latin America. He knew that his small body of troops would encounter hostile natives, unfriendly terrain, and tropical diseases. They would not want to persevere but instead would mutiny and go back to the ships they had come on and sail back to Spain, where they could enjoy relative comfort. To ensure their perseverance in the tasks set out before them, Cortés ordered that the ships be burned so that the troops could only go forward. The Christian singing group for KING & COUNTRY put out an amazing song entitled "Burn the Ships" based on that story.

The Lord lets His servants know that there is no room for retreat or defeat in His program. Jesus' disciples were filled with curiosity about whether their Lord was intending to establish an earthly kingdom. When would

He do it, and what time was His expected return? He told them very clearly, "It is not for you to know times or seasons which the Father has put in His own authority. But you shall receive power when the Holy Spirit has come upon you; and you shall be witnesses to Me in Jerusalem, and in all Judea and Samaria, and to the end of the earth."[1] As to the time of His second coming, He said that no man knew it, nor was it known to the angels of heaven. In fact, He, the Son of God, did not know the time or day.[2] To His disciples He gave the instruction, "Occupy till I come."[3] It is absolutely futile to spend great amounts of time speculating on events that foretell the future. Our task is to persevere until our Lord returns.

It takes time for certain events to materialize. Some things cannot be hurried. Think of the patience of the Creator, who waited fourteen billion years to see His universe take shape. Think of the hundreds of millions of years that God took to prepare our planet as a suitable dwelling place for human beings made in the image of God.[4]

First, our globe was a mass of flaming gas. Over hundreds of millions of years it cooled and solidified. Our planet needed water, and along the way, a giant comet made of frozen ice collided with our planet and filled the oceans with water. Then millions of years after that a planet (not unlike Mars) collided with our earth and ejected into space a small planet we know as the moon, which serves to stabilize our planet. Over the years geologic forces caused soil to cover parts of our earth, and then strikes by asteroids are thought to have carried seeds from various grains.

Little by little, the Creator God then brought forth on the earth various types of creatures and birds in the air and fish in the sea.

Over hundreds of millions of years the necessary minerals and gases to sustain life came into being. Only with careful perseverance did the Creator place upon our planet human beings with the command to "be fruitful and multiply; fill the earth and subdue it."[5] God is patient and allows His creation to reach the highest goals that He has set for it.

Think of the prophecy God made to Abraham that His people would be held in bondage by a foreign country until the time came for them to be redeemed and to return to the land promised to Abraham, Isaac, and Jacob. The Bible tells us "when the fullness of the time had come, God sent forth His Son, born of a woman, born under the law."[6] Think of the hundreds of years that elapsed from the time God led Abraham out of his family's dwelling into the Promised Land and then how long it took his heirs to form a nation and to be taught the oracles of God and God's righteous laws. Then, how long did it take for Israel to grow in the land and to receive the necessary promises that a Messiah would come and be called the Son of God? The prophet Habakkuk says, "The vision is yet for an appointed time.... Though it tarries, wait for it; because it will surely come."[7]

We persevere because we know that God has a perfect plan for His people and that plan will come to pass in His good time. According to Paul's letter to the Romans, God has a process that is available to each of us. It starts with faith, and then we are told that the trying of our faith produces endurance. In the Greek language is something called *onomatopoeia*, which means that the word somehow sounds like the action it represents, and we can almost hear the groan of somebody under a load of affliction carrying a heavy burden. But this endurance produces sterling character, and that in turn produces hope. And hope in turn is not ashamed—because the love of God is shed abroad in our hearts.

We have here the progression that God uses to bring about in each one of us the three cardinal Christian virtues: faith, hope, and love. Those who have faith can expect that faith to be tried in the furnace of affliction; as we persevere, we will gain proven character, and that character will teach us that we can rely on God. Once we truly have learned that we can trust Him, we no longer need to trust ourselves. And with that assurance our hearts reach out to love others. This is God's way to bring forth the Christian character, which can persevere regardless of the circumstances.

Before I finish this chapter, I need to point out a major problem in higher education, especially for adult learners. So many learners are faced with bewildering subject matters and requirements for skill in computer learning. It is so easy to drop out and miss the incredible opportunities that are offered to those with education.

When I was a youngster, I was enrolled in a music class that would teach me how to play the violin. I really hated it. I hated the instrument, and I hated the difficulty of learning various notes. I protested so vigorously that my indulgent mother allowed me to drop out of music education. Although I have a relatively fine sense to appreciate all forms of music, from country and western to classics, I still regret the fact that as a youngster I did not persevere in a skill that would have brought me much pleasure throughout my life, even to old age.

The Lord says, "No one, having put his hand to the plow, and looking back, is fit for the kingdom of God."[8] Jesus told a parable about a sower who went out to sow.[9] A sower went out to sow. Some of the seed fell on rocky ground and immediately sprang up, and when the sun came up, it withered and died. Some of the seed fell among thorns, and when the plants came up, they were choked out by the weeds and thorns. Some fell on good soil and brought forth thirty, sixty, and one hundred times the quantity of seeds sown.

When asked the meaning of this parable, Jesus explained to His disciples that the seeds sown on rocky ground pertain to Christians who have a shallow understanding of the truth of the gospel and are unable in themselves to persevere against difficult circumstances. These people fall away from the kingdom of God. Jesus said the seed that was sown among thorns represents those people who are filled with enthusiasm for the truth of the kingdom of God; however, they are so consumed with business and pleasure and the cares of this life that the fledgling seeds of the gospel of Christ are soon choked out, and they become unfruitful. Of course, the good soil represents those whose hearts have been prepared carefully to count the costs and to learn the truths of the gospel. They go forth and become very fruitful. The message here is very clear. What is called "cheap grace" won't do it. People have to be taught the principles of Christianity, they have to be prepared to surrender themselves, and they have to realize that the commitment to receive Jesus Christ as Savior means a lifetime of service and perseverance against all odds.

Such people are described in the Book of Hebrews as those who take kingdoms, who shut the mouths of lions, who live a life of resurrected power, and who are fully committed to entering a holy city "whose builder and maker is God."[10]

CHAPTER 8

THE LAW OF FIDELITY

THE BIBLE SAYS that it is required of the servant that he be faithful. Without question, fidelity (faithfulness) is a key attribute of someone who would please God. Here's how Jesus described it.[1] A man entrusted his possessions to one of his officials with instructions that he should provide sustenance for each of his servants. Jesus then said, "Blessed is that servant whom his master will find so doing" when the Lord returns.[2] So, fidelity in the secret kingdom involves serving spiritual nourishment to God's family while we wait for the return of Jesus.

However, Jesus gave this warning when the master found that his trusted overseer had gotten drunk, was neglecting his responsibilities, and actually had begun to mistreat his subordinates. The Lord said the master would find the servant and in anger would "cut him in two and appoint him his portion with the unbelievers."[3]

The message for us is clear. We must not presume upon the goodness of the Lord and in our daily life engage in carnality and abuse of others. I hear so often that people rely on the doctrine "once saved, always saved." This may sound comforting, but it clearly must be qualified by other teachings in the Bible.

In John's Gospel 5:24, Jesus says, "He who hears My word and believes in Him who sent Me has everlasting life, and shall not come into judgment, but has passed from death into life." What judgment is Jesus talking about? He is speaking of the judgment described in Revelation as the great white throne where those not written in the Book of Life are being cast into eternal damnation.[4] This is undoubtedly the preferred meaning of that statement.

However, the Bible tells us that everyone shall give an account of his or her actions. Jesus tells us of servants who did not know the Lord's will who because of their sin were beaten with few stripes. Those who knew the Lord's will and still sinned were beaten with many stripes.[5]

The apostle Paul describes what in Greek is called the *bema*, or the judgment seat of Christ. To account for things that we have done in our body obviously would be patently unfair if one person who said he was a born-again Christian and who lived a life of indifference and carelessness received the same reward as someone who dedicated his life to acts of kindness and charity toward others. Isn't this what Jesus was talking about when He spoke of a time when He, as final Judge, was separating sheep from goats?[6]

To the sheep He said, "Come, you blessed of My Father, inherit the kingdom prepared for you from the foundation of the world: for I was hungry and you gave Me food; I was thirsty and you gave Me drink; I was a stranger and you took Me in; I was naked and you clothed Me; I was sick and you visited Me; I was in prison and you came to Me."[7] And they said to Him, "Lord, when did we see You hungry and feed You, or thirsty and give You drink? When did we see You a stranger and take You in, or naked and clothe

You? Or when did we see You sick, or in prison, and come to You?"[8] And He said, "Inasmuch as you did it to one of the least of these My brethren, you did it to Me.[9] Come, you blessed of My Father, inherit the kingdom prepared for you from the foundation of the world."[10]

Then to the goats He said, "I was hungry and you gave Me no food; I was thirsty and you gave Me no drink; I was a stranger and you did not take Me in, naked and you did not clothe Me, sick and in prison and you did not visit Me."[11] Again they asked, "Lord, when did we see You hungry or thirsty or a stranger or naked or sick or in prison, and did not minister to You?"[12] And Jesus said to them, "Inasmuch as you did not do it to one of the least of these, you did not do it to Me. Depart from Me, you cursed, into the everlasting fire prepared for the devil and his angels."[13]

There are three groups spoken of here: sheep, goats, and brethren. Who are the brethren? Is Jesus referring to His Christian brothers and sisters? Or is He referring to His fellow Jews? In this parable Jesus is clearly saying that, among other things, the eternal destiny of the unsaved will depend on their treatment of those referred to as His brethren.

To sum up what these scriptures are teaching, first of all, out of the billions of people in the world, those who believe the gospel and who have repented of their sins and claim Jesus as their Savior will not face the terrible white throne judgment that is spoken of in the Book of Revelation. But somehow along the way, a measure of the severity of the punishment of the ungodly will be determined by their treatment of those who are either the believers in Jesus Christ or members of the Jewish race.

Finally, without question, those of us who are disciples of Jesus and have received His transforming Spirit will receive rewards commensurate with the kindness that we have shown and our obedience to His commands during our lifetime, as was said so eloquently in the Book of Daniel: "Those who are wise shall shine like the brightness of the firmament, and those who turn many to righteousness like the stars forever and ever."[14]

BE FAITHFUL TO ONE ANOTHER

Bringing these teachings closer to home, when two people enter into a marriage contract, it is absolutely essential that they abide by the terms of that agreement and that they be faithful to one another. The Law of Fidelity demands that a wife be faithful to her husband and that a husband be faithful to his wife.

In like manner, an employee who agrees to serve in either a business or nonprofit entity must be faithful. Whatever the legal ramifications, I am frankly appalled at a trusted employee in a federal agency who will undermine the leadership of that agency and leak confidential information to the enemies of his or her employer.

The attorney-client privilege demands fidelity. Author John Grisham wrote a fascinating novel called *The Firm* that was made into a very exciting motion picture starring

Tom Cruise, and the central feature was the sanctity of the attorney-client privilege.

I am a Baptist, but I certainly feel that the Catholic sacrament of confession is an excellent catharsis for those troubled by their sins. Nevertheless the priest owes a sacred obligation not to reveal the secrets from the confessional.

When I was serving as an interim pastor in a Baptist church, a few of the parishioners came to me for counseling and confided in me their secrets. I refused to divulge these secrets, even to my wife. Later on, one of the women was talking to my wife and said, "You mean Pat didn't tell you about this?" And my wife said, "No, I never heard anything about it." As a minister I had to be faithful to the Lord and to those who trusted their confidential information to me.

How terrible it is to find a wife who shares gossip with her friends about her husband's behavior in the bedroom. Fidelity means that you don't cheat on one another mentally, spiritually, or physically.

It is absolutely sinful to tell lies about someone or to reveal his or her innermost secrets. Never having been a teenage girl, I can't imagine the humiliation that comes to such a child when a parent breaks faith and reveals the child's secret hopes, dreams, or romantic crush.

We are called upon to be faithful to one another—to our friends, to our business associates, and to our suppliers. In today's business there seems to be an incredible lack of trust, so companies protect themselves by having voluminous contracts drawn up filled with legalese that few, if any, can understand.

However, one of my business dealings was with a fabulously wealthy media mogul named Rupert Murdoch. As we were speaking of one matter, Rupert said, "I give you my word." To me, that was all I needed. I valued the word of a man of integrity much more than I valued the hundred-page contract drafted by a Wall Street lawyer.

CHAPTER 9

THE LAW OF CHANGE

Another eternal principle in the secret kingdom I call the Law of Change. Jesus said that nobody will "put new wine into old wineskins, or else the wineskins break, the wine is spilled, and the wineskins are ruined. But they put new wine into new."[1] What is the spiritual meaning of this teaching?

Human institutions, like old wineskins, become brittle and often are subject to cracking. People involved are set in their ways, and they love the phrase "We have always done it this way."

It has been said that those who think they know God always persecute those who really do. Contemplate the historic record when Martin Luther nailed his Ninety-Five Theses to the door of the church in Wittenberg. He was merely trying to be a good Catholic and offer suggestions to bring about peaceful reform. Instead he was excommunicated and hunted down as an outlaw by the ecclesiastical hierarchy.

When John Calvin gained ecclesiastical control of Geneva, he permitted the drowning of those known as Anabaptists, who felt that being sprinkled as unbelievers was inadequate and wanted to be baptized by immersion as believers.

King Henry VIII, who was less concerned with church doctrine than the pursuit of women and wealth, repudiated the authority of the pope of the Roman Catholic Church and established himself as the head of the Church of England, executing anyone who stood in his way.

In the modern era, Charismatics and Pentecostals were persecuted by Baptists and more Protestant denominations because the old skins could not accommodate the new wine that the Holy Spirit was pouring out throughout the world.

Henry Ford was considered a brilliant inventor, but he was fixated on the manufacturing of his black, stripped-down Model T automobile. When his son, Edsel, had created a shiny, sleek Model A car, it was reported that his father took a sledgehammer and broke the beautiful new car to pieces.

The brilliant Thomas Edison put together an electrical system dependent on direct current; he rejected the alternating current proposed by Tesla. The ultimate conflict resulted in Edison losing control of his company to a syndicate formed by banker J. P. Morgan.

To most people, "the old way is always better."

New Wine

When I first came to the Tidewater, Virginia, area with a mandate from God to start a Christian television station, I went before the ministerial council to attempt to gain their support. After I had made my presentation about how wonderful a Christian television station would be, I stepped outside the main room. While in a waiting room, I overheard the conversation of the assembled clergy. One statement still resonates in my mind: "If we can't stop it, at least we can disassociate ourselves from it." What I was proposing was a vastly new way of reaching people with the gospel and of bringing the message into the homes of people. Traditional churches at that time wanted nothing to do with it because they felt this technology would be disruptive to their Sunday services.

Later on I was told by one minister, "If you can give up all this business about the Holy Spirit, then you can get Baptist support." What God had in me was new wine— new worship, new methods of preaching the gospel, and a return to the worship of the first century.

I formed The Christian Broadcasting Network. My initial capital was $70. I had to struggle to accomplish what God had placed inside me. But if I had tried to link my vision with existing church life, I would have ruined them, and they would have ruined what we had in mind. It took considerable struggle to stay free and independent, but the anointing of the Holy Spirit was powerful. As the years went by, the new wine that our work represented became perhaps the most powerful evangelistic tool in the entire world. We produce programs in over 80 languages, which are seen in over 150 countries and territories around the world. We have powerful motion pictures, a news channel, various avenues on the internet, and broadcasts that over the years have resulted in at least one billion people receiving Jesus Christ as their Savior.

Imagine what I would have given up had I forsaken the power of God to gain Baptist support or to alter our broadcast techniques so as not to offend the local Sunday church services of a few small churches in Tidewater, Virginia.

What is now known as the Charismatic movement is the fastest-growing religious expression in the world, with at least six hundred million adherents, well on the way to one billion. There is no way that any existing church structure could have accommodated the move of God that is now sweeping the world.

Change for change is not the answer. I am a firm believer in the maxim "If it ain't broke, don't fix it." If something is functioning well, we would certainly want to support it. But at the same time, we recognize that dramatic inventions—whether the steam engine or power looms or locomotives or automobiles or airplanes or the current level of work done by robots—will be opposed by those who feel threatened by innovation.

French peasants wore wooden shoes called *sabots*. It is alleged that when peasants felt that machinery was taking away their employment, they began to throw their shoes into the gears of the machines. Some say that's how we got the word *sabotage*. Whether that's an urban legend or not, even today I'm reading of a resistance by labor unions at job-saving automation that is taking away the jobs of unskilled laborers. But like it or not, we cannot resist the Law of Change and the simple truth that new wine cannot be poured into old wineskins, lest the skins break and the wine be lost.[2]

CHAPTER 10

THE LAW OF DOMINION

IN THE BOOK of Genesis we read that when God created mankind, He blessed them and gave them this mandate: "Be fruitful and multiply; fill the earth and subdue it; have dominion over the fish of the sea, over the birds of the air, and over every living thing that moves on the earth."[1]

This dominion obviously extended to serpents, and we are told that in the Garden of Eden a serpent appeared to Eve with a question: "Has God indeed said, 'You shall not eat of every tree of the garden'?"[2]

Now, keep in mind that God had placed everything in the garden that was delightful to taste and smell and enjoy. It was truly a garden of delights. And yet God had reserved one thing for the purpose of training His newly formed creatures. They had to be taught some type of moral rectitude. How did He go about doing it? He placed in the garden one tree that was called the tree of the knowledge of good and evil. And God said, "Of every tree of the garden you may freely eat; but of the tree of the knowledge of good and evil you shall not eat."[3] So when Adam and Eve were to go by this tree, they could tell themselves, "If we eat from this tree, it is wrong and sinful. If we refrain from eating the fruit of this tree, it is righteous and holy." Every day, when they went by the tree, they would learn the knowledge of good and evil.

Theologians in the Middle Ages used the term *posse non peccare*, which means "able to not sin,"[4] for those who essentially were morally neutral. In short, there was no compulsion to sin for the young couple in the Garden of Eden. But after a period of time a habit of righteousness would be developed; the theologians call that *non posse peccare*, or "not able to sin."[5] In short, after weeks of obedience had gone by, the habit of obedience would be so ingrained that not only would it become natural; it would be impossible for them to sin.

However, Satan wanted to break that virtuous cycle of obedience, so he entered as the serpent, over which God had given Adam and Eve dominion, in order to take away their dominion. Satan found a flaw in Eve's thinking when she said, "Yes, there's one tree in the garden from which we can't eat its fruit or even touch it."[6] This one mistake let Satan realize that Eve had a fatal flaw. To this he then contradicted God's express command and said, "You will not surely die."[7] Then Eve's spirit began to think that God was holding something good away from her, so she reached out and took the fruit of the tree of the knowledge of good and evil.

When Eve ate the fruit, she lost the dominion that God had given her. She offered the fruit to her husband, and he ate it. As the "federal head" of the human race, Adam and his wife were expelled from the Garden of Eden, lost paradise, and lost the dominion that God had given them over all the earth.

It was not until the time of Jesus Christ, when He lived

a perfectly sinless life and became the second Adam, that the human race restored what it had lost in the Garden of Eden. He brought His disciples to Himself and said to them, "All authority has been given to Me in heaven and on earth. Go therefore and make disciples of all the nations, baptizing them in the name of the Father and of the Son and of the Holy Spirit, teaching them to observe all things that I have commanded you; and lo, I am with you always, even to the end of the age."[8]

EXERCISE YOUR DOMINION

The authority that Jesus gave to His disciples extends to sickness, disease, finances, demonic power, and all created beings. The dominion we enjoy flows from our relationship to the Son of God who says, "All [and I repeat, *all*] authority has been given to Me in heaven and on earth,"[9] and as His representatives, we go forth with a mandate of unlimited power. However, as in the Garden of Eden, Satan will exercise every device to cause us to break the bond that we have with our heavenly Father.

The story is told in the Old Testament about Balak, king of Moab, who saw the Israelites marching into his land.[10] In fear he sent representatives to a prophet named Balaam to offer Balaam a huge sum of money to come and curse the children of Israel. Balaam at first refused the emissaries of the king of Moab but then went back to the Lord to get a second opinion. This time he received permission to go. Even on his way, an angel with a drawn sword stood in his way and attempted to kill him.

Balaam ascended a high hill, and after performing a ritual sacrifice, he began a pronouncement. Yet what came out of his mouth was a blessing. For a second and third time Balak came to him and said, "I took you to curse my enemies, and look, you have blessed them bountifully!"[11] Then Balaam brought forth a beautiful song of praise that forcefully declared that there could be no curse against the nation that God Almighty had blessed. "How lovely are your tents, O Jacob! Your dwellings, O Israel!...His king shall be higher than Agag, and his kingdom shall be exalted."[12] With this Balaam retired from the high place, and Balak shook his head in disgust and said, in effect, "I would have enriched you and given you much honor, but now you have betrayed me."[13]

The lesson here is clear: as long as Israel was pleasing God, no evil force or curse could come against them. The problem is that Satan was not finished; he realized that to defeat Israel he had to break Israel's connection to the God of the universe. So how did he do it? He flooded the Israelite camp with sensual Moabite women who held to the same promiscuity that was forbidden to God's holy people but was commonplace among the heathen who lived in that part of the world.

One notable occurrence concerned Cozbi, the daughter of a Midianite prince, who began an act of fornication with one of the leading Israelites in his tent right in the middle of the congregation. Phinehas, one of the sons of Levi, was so infuriated that he took a spear and drove it through the back of the Israelite and through the stomach of the Midianite woman. The Lord was so pleased with this act of obedience that He promoted Phinehas to a special place in His temple and stopped the plague that had been spreading among the people who had surrendered their power and dominion because they had broken the commands of God.[14]

The principle is very simple. You and I must be aware of the grant of dominion that has come to us through the Lord Jesus Christ. Then we must exercise that dominion, or it will do us no good. We must be ever diligent to continue to do the will of God lest He withdraw His grant of authority.

THE ATTACK ON OUR DOMINION

According to the *World Drug Report 2019*, the United Nations' overview of the global extent of drug use, 188 million people around the world use cannabis; 53 million use opioids (with 29 million of these using opiates such as heroin and opium); 29 million use amphetamines and prescription stimulants; 21 million use ecstasy; and 18 million use cocaine.[15] Just think, human beings made in the image of God who have been given authority over all the earth to subdue it are themselves the slaves of fermented corn water, fermented rye water, ground-up poppies, and ground-up coca leaves. Isn't it horrible to contemplate the millions of dollars that our society could be spending on noble pursuits that must be spent in the rehabilitation of human beings made in God's image who have allowed themselves to be the bondslaves of fruits and vegetables?

However, our dominion as children of God is also under attack from a system that seems intent on expanding the rate of incarceration in our nation. It's a tragic fact that in this supposedly free, democratic society in which we live, we have more men and women incarcerated than Communist China or Communist Russia has.[16] Not only are there thousands of federal statutory crimes, but there are also several hundred thousand criminal penalties assessed by federal administrative agencies.

On *The 700 Club*, we produced a series of very powerful programs referring to America as a "Nation of Criminals." The term *penitentiary* has its roots in the term *penitent*, which means feeling sorrow and repentance. Instead of this, most penitentiaries become schools of crime. Inmates, when their service is completed, often go out as skilled criminals rather than repentant sinners.

Regrettably, thousands of people involved in law enforcement are able to adjust the facts before them in order to secure confessions and later convictions. One particularly egregious case had to do with a woman named Valerie Plame who was employed by the CIA. In a newspaper column, she was identified as a CIA employee. As I understand it, it is a federal offense to publicly identify a CIA agent who is working undercover in a foreign nation. I do not believe it is any offense to identify an employee of the CIA who is working for the government in Washington, DC. Nevertheless, when a newspaper reporter mentioned that Valerie Plame was a CIA employee, a massive federal investigation was set in motion to identify the source of the leak.

A zealous prosecutor named Patrick Fitzgerald began proceedings. Fairly early on in his investigation he learned that the source of the leak was an official in the State Department. Fitzgerald apparently did not reveal his knowledge but began detailed questioning under oath of a lawyer named Scooter Libby who was an assistant to Vice President Dick Cheney. From what I have learned, Scooter Libby had no firsthand knowledge of the identity of Valerie Plame. Even if he had known, again, revealing a Washington-based CIA agent, to the best of my knowledge, is not a federal offense. Nevertheless, under intense questioning, Scooter Libby gave answers that the prosecutor alleged were perjurious. So, this fine man was prosecuted for perjury and convicted. He lost his law license and his public standing because a zealous prosecutor wanted to take his dominion away from him. To his shame, George W. Bush refused to pardon Scooter Libby, but finally, Donald Trump did.

Another egregious example of prosecutorial overreach occurred in the case of Martha Stewart. Martha was a billionaire and had bought some stock in a medical start-up company named ImClone. From what I gather, Martha Stewart had a perfect right to own the stock and was in no way guilty of insider trading for the small amount of stock she owned. Nevertheless, under intense questioning she gave the FBI what was alleged to be perjury, and she was sent to prison for a short period of time.

At Regent University there is a very brilliant criminal law professor named James Duane. As he surveyed the extraordinary traps that were set out by law enforcement, his recommendation to anybody accused of a violation was to repeatedly claim the Fifth Amendment for protection against self-incrimination—in all cases and at all times.[17] What Professor Duane would be quick to ask us all is why any one of us would put a weapon in a prosecutor's hands that would rob us of our dominion as a child of God and citizen of this great nation.

DOMINION IS NOT DIVISION

The grant of dominion extends to the entire human race. But we must recognize that dominion must be tempered when dealing with individual human beings. In every enterprise, including a family, there must be one head. Jesus said, "No one can serve two masters; for either he will hate the one and love the other, or else he will be loyal to the one and despise the other."[18]

In giving humanity dominion over the earth, God did not intend to set up a power struggle between individual people. Children are supposed to obey their parents, who are in turn to bring them up in the nurture and admonition of the Lord. A husband is supposed to love his wife as he loves his own body and care for her as Jesus Christ cares for the church. However, a wife is supposed to acknowledge that her husband is the head of the family even as

Christ is head of the husband. We are directed to give honor to whom honor is due and allegiance to whom allegiance is due. Especially in marriages, the husband is to be the head of the family, and frankly, it is incumbent upon the wife to make him the head. If wives refuse to submit to their husbands or if they attempt to take authority over them, then it won't take much time before the husband is seeking some outlet with another woman or is seeking a divorce. I have spoken before about the Law of Unity, and without question, a divided house is intolerable and will sooner or later come to ruin.

Regrettably, men who drink to excess and who squander their earnings on frivolity will have lost the headship that the Bible gives them as the normal order of things. We read the story of Mary and Joseph and learn that an angel appeared to Joseph in a dream and instructed him to take Mary and the young baby, Jesus, and flee to Egypt because Herod was seeking to kill the male infants of Bethlehem. We also learn that the Holy Spirit spoke to Joseph in Egypt and told him that he could now return to Israel and that he should settle in a town called Nazareth.[19] It is clear to me that even though Mary was chosen as the mother of Jesus, the Lord and the angels followed the natural order of authority and directed the family through the husband, not through the wife.

RESPONSIBILITY AND THE LAW OF DOMINION

I have found a wonderful organization called Opportunity International, which makes microenterprise loans to poor people all over the world. A microenterprise loan would enable a woman to buy a sewing machine or the produce necessary to open a small store, to buy leather to resole shoes, or to buy material to make dresses, and so on. This wonderful company brings together groups of women and, in that circle of women, makes a few of these small loans. Then the women are responsible to use the money to build a small enterprise, and the entire group monitors each other to make sure that there are no defaults on the loans. The reason to give to the women instead of the men is simple. The men in so many developing countries waste money on frivolity, alcohol, and gambling to such a degree that no responsible lender would advance them money. On the other hand, the women have nearly a 100 percent rate of paying back loans and with their diligence become credit worthy for increasing amounts. These men obviously have been given dominion, but it seems in each of these cases they have surrendered their dominion to their wives.

To recap, those of us who know Jesus have been given extraordinary authority. We are to be in charge of this world—but true leaders must not only be in charge; they must also be responsible for what they do. Those who know the Lord will not pollute the rivers, will not clearcut the forests, will not decimate the fish and the wildlife, and certainly will not pollute the air. We do not embrace a scheme of international control over our lives, but each one of us will take every opportunity available to care for this planet on which we live so that it will not only be fresh and clean for us but will also be a legacy for our children and our children's children.

EPILOGUE

As I SAID in the beginning of this book, I have learned that when Jesus Christ, who is the Son of God, makes a clear statement that is not limited to time, place, or recipient, that statement becomes a fundamental law that is as powerful as the law of gravity.

In this small book I have set out for you ten principles and application of those principles, which, if followed, can bring your family blessing and economic success.

With these ten laws, you will be carried along in a current of rich blessing. If you ignore them, you will be fighting upstream during your life.

The words of Jesus Christ ring true: "Therefore whoever hears these sayings of Mine, and does them, I will liken him to a wise man who built his house on the rock: and the rain descended, the floods came, and the winds blew and beat on that house; and it did not fall, for it was founded on the rock. But everyone who hears these sayings of Mine, and does not do them, will be like a foolish man who built his house on the sand: and the rain descended, the floods came, and the winds blew and beat on that house; and it fell."[1]

The apostle Paul said it this way: "As a wise master builder I have laid the foundation . . . which is Jesus Christ. Now if anyone builds on this foundation with gold, silver, precious stones, wood, hay, straw, each one's work will become clear; for the Day will declare it, because it will be revealed by fire; and the fire will test each one's work, of what sort it is. If anyone's work which he has built on it endures, he will receive a reward."[2]

POSTSCRIPT

My dear friend Chauncey Crandall is a world-renowned cardiologist and the Director of Preventive Medicine and Complex Cardiology at Mount Sinai Heart Hospital in Palm Beach, Florida. He pointed out to me that the words of the apostle Paul declared that "the law of the Spirit of life" is in Christ Jesus, and the rabbinical regulations constituted "the law of sin and death."[3] These are two laws not included in my book, but I add them as an interesting postscript.

NOTES

PREFACE

1. James Kirchick, "Carter's Role in Zimbabwe," *New York Sun*, July 11, 2007, https://www.nysun.com/opinion/carters-role-in-zimbabwe/58232/.

2. United States Congress, House Committee on Foreign Affairs, Subcommittee on Western Hemisphere Affairs, *"Hearing Before the Subcommittee on Western Hemisphere Affairs of the Committee on Foreign Affairs House of Representatives, Ninety-Ninth Congress, First Session, April 16, 17, and 18, 1985"* (Washington, DC: US Government Printing Office, 1985), 19.

3. Elaine Kamarck, "The Iranian Hostage Crisis and Its Effect on American Politics," Brookings, November 4, 2019, https://www.brookings.edu/blog/order-from-chaos/2019/11/04/the-iranian-hostage-crisis-and-its-effect-on-american-politics/.

4. A televised speech delivered by President Carter on July 15, 1979, came to be known as his "malaise speech," although Carter never actually used the word *malaise* in the speech. See "Examining Carter's 'Malaise Speech,' Thirty Years Later," NPR, July 12, 2009, https://www.npr.org/templates/story/story.php?storyId=106508243.

CHAPTER 1: THE LAW OF USE

1. See Matthew 25:14–30.

2. Luke 19:13, KJV.

3. Matt. 25:24–25, author's paraphrase.

4. Matt. 25:21.

5. Matt. 25:23.

6. Matt. 25:24–25, author's paraphrase.

7. Matt. 25:26–28, author's paraphrase.

8. Matt 25:29, author's paraphrase.

9. Matt. 25:26, KJV.

10. "Weekly National Rates and Rate Caps—Weekly Update,"
    Federal Deposit Insurance Corporation, last updated November
    25, 2019, https://www.fdic.gov/regulations/resources/rates/.

11. Matt. 25:26, KJV.

12. Ken Bossone, *Why Positive Thinkers Have the Power: How to
    Use the Powerful Three-Word Motto to Achieve Greater Peace
    of Mind* (Hollywood, FL: Frederick Fell, 2008), https://books.
    google.com/books?id=mT1w2elYoDoC&pg.

13. "Ignacy Jan Paderewski Quotes and Sayings," Inspiring Quotes,
    accessed December 1, 2019, https://www.inspiringquotes.us/
    author/3263-ignacy-jan-paderewski.

14. Matt. 25:29, author's paraphrase.

15. Michael Cannivet, "How Einstein Would Manage His Portfolio,"
    Forbes, December 7, 2017, https://www.forbes.com/sites/
    michaelcannivet/2017/12/07/how-einstein-would-manage-his-
    portfolio/#fd4a65b12b2b.

16. Anneken Tappe, "Three Reasons to Fear America's Massive $70
    Trillion Debt Pile," CNN Business, July 17, 2019, https://www.
    cnn.com/2019/07/17/investing/united-states-debt-risks/index.
    html.

17. Martin Crutsinger, "2019 US Federal Budget Deficit Surges
    to Nearly $1 Trillion, the Highest in Seven Years," *USA
    Today*, October 25, 2019, https://www.usatoday.com/story/
    money/2019/10/25/rising-national-debt-2019-us-budget-deficit-
    nearly-1-trillion/2458452001/.

18. David John, "Misleading the Public: How the Social Security
    Trust Fund Really Works," The Heritage Foundation, September
    2, 2004, https://www.heritage.org/social-security/report/
    misleading-the-public-how-the-social-security-trust-fund-really-
    works.

19. Prov. 5:18, TLV.

20. 1 John 4:7.

21. Prov. 17:22.

CHAPTER 2: THE LAW OF RECIPROCITY

1. Eckardt C. Beck, "The Love Canal Tragedy," US Environmental Protection Agency, January 1979, https://archive.epa.gov/epa/aboutepa/love-canal-tragedy.html.

2. Beck, "The Love Canal Tragedy."

3. Beck, "The Love Canal Tragedy."

4. Fred Schulte, "How Rival Opioid Makers Sought to Cash In on Alarm Over OxyContin's Dangers," Kaiser Health News, August 2, 2018, https://www.statnews.com/2018/08/02/rival-opioid-makers-oxycontin-dangers/.

5. Joanna Walters, "Meet the Sacklers: The Family Feuding Over Blame for the Opioid Crisis," *Guardian*, February 13, 2018, https://www.theguardian.com/us-news/2018/feb/13/meet-the-sacklers-the-family-feuding-over-blame-for-the-opioid-crisis.

6. Steven Reinberg, "Opioid Dependence Can Start in Just a Few Days," WebMD, March 16, 2017, https://www.webmd.com/mental-health/addiction/news/20170316/opioid-dependence-can-start-in-just-a-few-days#1.

7. Luke 6:38.

8. Mal. 3:10.

9. Mal. 3:10.

10. John Becklake, "Secrets of the Reich's Rocket Man," NewScientist, December 17, 1994, https://www.newscientist.com/article/mg14419564-500-secrets-of-the-reichs-rocket-man/.

11. Prov. 15:1.

12. Luke 7:29.

13. Devan Cole, "Buttigieg to Pence: 'If You Got a Problem With Who I Am, Your Problem Is Not With Me—Your Quarrel, Sir, Is With My Creator,'" CNN, updated April 8, 2019, https://www.cnn.com/2019/04/08/politics/pete-buttigieg-mike-pence/index.html.

CHAPTER 3: THE LAW OF RESPONSIBILITY

1. Luke 12:48.
2. Luke 17:10.
3. See, for example, 1 Kings 2:10; 11:21, 43; 2 Kings 8:24; 10:35, all in the NIV.
4. See 1 Corinthians 6:3.

CHAPTER 4: THE LAW OF GREATNESS

1. Mark 10:42–44.
2. John 13:13–14.
3. See Philippians 2:5–8.
4. "1960s: Retail Revolution," Walmart Digital Museum, accessed December 1, 2019, https://walmartmuseum.auth.cap-hosting.com/tour/decade-intros/1960/.
5. George Vecsey, "Wooden as a Teacher: The First Lesson Was Shoelaces," *New York Times*, June 4, 2010, https://www.nytimes.com/2010/06/05/sports/ncaabasketball/05wizard.html.
6. See Matthew 20:26 and Mark 10:44.

CHAPTER 5: THE LAW OF MIRACLES

1. See Mark 11:12–24.
2. Mark 11:14.
3. Mark 11:21.
4. Mark 11:22.
5. Heb. 11:6.
6. Heb. 11:1.
7. See James 1:6–8.
8. Rom. 4:20–21.
9. Prov. 13:2.
10. Mark 11:14.
11. See Mark 11:22–23.
12. Mark 11:23.

13. See Mark 11:23.
14. Matt. 6:12.
15. Mark 11:25.

CHAPTER 6: THE LAW OF UNITY

1. Gen. 11:1, 6, NIV.
2. See Matthew 12:25.
3. Gen. 11:6, NIV.

CHAPTER 7: THE LAW OF PERSEVERANCE

1. Acts 1:7–8.
2. See Matthew 24:36 and Mark 13:32.
3. Luke 19:13, KJV.
4. The Bible says that God created the earth in six days. Our days are twenty-four hours, but what is a day for God? The Bible says that a day with the Lord is a thousand years, and a thousand years is a day. It does no violence to Scripture to believe that a Creator-day could be as much as a billion earth years.
5. Gen. 1:28.
6. Gal. 4:4.
7. Hab. 2:3.
8. Luke 9:62.
9. See Matthew 13:1–23, Mark 4:1–20, and Luke 8:4–15.
10. Heb. 11:10, 33–35.

CHAPTER 8: THE LAW OF FIDELITY

1. See Matthew 24:45–51 and Luke 12:42–48.
2. Luke 12:43.
3. Luke 12:46.
4. See Revelation 20:11–15.
5. See Luke 12:42–48.
6. See Matthew 25:31–46.

7. Matt. 25:34–36.
8. Matt. 25:37–39.
9. Matt. 25:40.
10. Matt. 25:34.
11. Matt. 25:42–43.
12. Matt. 25:44.
13. Matt. 25:45, 41.
14. Dan. 12:3.

CHAPTER 9: THE LAW OF CHANGE

1. Matt. 9:17.
2. Matt. 9:17.

CHAPTER 10: THE LAW OF DOMINION

1. Gen. 1:28.
2. Gen. 3:1.
3. Gen. 2:16–17.
4. R. C. Sproul, "Radical Corruption," Ligonier Ministries, accessed December 1, 2019, https://www.ligonier.org/learn/articles/radical-corruption/.
5. Sproul, "Radical Corruption."
6. Gen. 3:2–3, author's paraphrase.
7. Gen. 3:4.
8. Matt. 28:18–20.
9. Matt. 28:18.
10. See Numbers 22–24.
11. Num. 23:11.
12. Num. 24:5, 7.
13. See Numbers 24:11.
14. See Numbers 25:6–13.

15. United Nations Office on Drugs and Crime, *World Drug Report 2019*, June 2019, https://wdr.unodc.org/wdr2019/prelaunch/WDR19_Booklet_1_EXECUTIVE_SUMMARY.pdf.

16. "World Prison Populations," BBC News, accessed December 2, 2019, http://news.bbc.co.uk/2/shared/spl/hi/uk/06/prisons/html/nn2page1.stm.

17. James Duane, "Don't Talk to the Police," Regent University School of Law, posted March 20, 2012, YouTube video, 46:38, https://www.youtube.com/watch?v=d-7o9xYp7eE.

18. Matt. 6:24.

19. See Matthew 2:13–15, 19–21.

Epilogue

1. Matt. 7:24–27.

2. 1 Cor. 3:10–14.

3. Rom. 8:2.